Last Train to Paris

Last Train to Paris

a group novel

Published by

a graduating course of English

Kurt-Tucholsky-Schule

Bibliographical Information of the Deutsche Nationalbibliothek
This publication is listed in the Deutsche Nationalbibliographie of the Deutsche
Nationalbibliothek; detailed bibliographical information can be accessed under
http: //dnb.d-nb.de

© 2013 Kurt-Tucholsky-Schule
Printing, Production and Layout: BoD – Books on Demand
ISBN: 978-3-7322-2665-8

Inhalt

INTRODUCTION 7

CHAPTER 1 9

CHAPTER 2 12

CHAPTER 3 15

CHAPTER 4 18

CHAPTER 5 21

CHAPTER 6 25

CHAPTER 7 27

CHAPTER 8 30

CHAPTER 9 33

CHAPTER 10 36

CHAPTER 11 38

CHAPTER 12 42

CHAPTER 13 44

CHAPTER 14 47

CHAPTER 15 50

CHAPTER 16 54

CHAPTER 17 57

CHAPTER 18 62

CHAPTER 19 **64**

CHAPTER 20 **66**

INTRODUCTION

This novel was written by my graduating class of English at a German school in Hamburg. Each year every class has to read a novel, in 2012 it was a novel written by a 17-year-old. This was when the idea came to my mind. When I asked my class whether they would like to try writing a novel themselves they immediately said 'yes'. I told them right away that it would mean a lot of work besides the regular coursework but they were quite enthusiastic.

There is no question about it, it was very hard work. We needed to agree on an outline of the plot so several people could work on different chapters at the same time. Others were doing some necessary research or working on the first drafts or proof reading. Researching, writing and rewriting, typing, correcting, and again rewriting and typing – everybody worked very hard but we also had a lot of fun. Of course there were times when we came close to abandoning the project but the hope that one day it would be done and the school would finance the print made us go on.

These are the students of the course

Back row from left to right: Zeleihka Foladi, Jimmy Brüning, Robert Oestmann, Torben Wißmeyer, Eren Ime, Mohammed Ponten, Yasin Özdemir.

Front row from left to right: Maria Jark, Nafize Karacelik, Aisha Saddika, Bedirhan Alimoglu, Oguzhan Maras, Evgenia Kyrlidou, Vanessa Bilardo, Esra Dede, Anica Tolic, Seher Canbolat, Gianna Paschburg.

Kneeling in front: Elham Rahmani, Hayat Starken.

We want to thank Mr. Seifert, another teacher at our school, for reading correction our final draft and Mr Gudjons for readily finding a possibility to finance the print.

Catharina Benzmann

CHAPTER 1

Nick was hungry. As he was sitting on the bed in his tiny room he couldn't think straight because of his merciless hunger. His four walls didn't offer much to do. On the left side was his bed made out of straw and on the opposite side, just below the rarely cleaned window, was his desk which was full of books about geography, history and culture. He was a real book-worm, who read everyhing that the library of Mr. Bence, just two crossroads away, had to offer. His closet was not really a closet, but an old cupboard which his mother had given him to put away the few clothes he had. Nick lived in a big but not very clean house. The family did not have enough money and time to take care of the house. The grass wasn't green like the grass at the neighbor's and it did not grow in every place. The color of the wall was a bit dark and looked really dirty. One could not see that the color of the house had been nearly white once. At the base some bricks were missing. And if one took a careful look one could see that moss was in the rainwater gutter. The reason why the house was so neglected was that the family had just time to get enough money to pay the mortgage but not to take care of it. Compared to Nick's surrounding area the house didn't fit. Those houses there were clean and their owners took care of them or had somebody who did this.

A sudden tremendous rumble out of his stomach broke the silence and he felt that he was starving. Inconspiciously he went downstairs entertaining the hope of finding a bountiful table with his family sitting around it. But his expectations were, as always, not fulfilled. On the worn-out kitchen table that looked the years it had been in use was nothing but two slices of bread, some cheese and a little note which said: "I'm in town with your sister – love Mum." As he sat and ate he looked out of the kitchen window and suddenly a sunray illuminated the grey room. He enjoyed the warm sun smiling at his face, and felt a little better than before.

An unfamiliar noise which he could not identify reached Nick's ears. That must be the biggest car he ever heard. He was curious and tried to sneak a peek through the window. A huge blue truck came up his street and stopped about 100 feet away, directly in front of Mr. Sander's house, who had moved to Kentucky in order to open up his own restaurant. A very expensive-looking black car with matten windows stopped just behind the big truck. Nick went into the living room to get a better look at what was happening. The passenger door of the car opened and a strong-looking man with a black suit and short hair came out. He looked like the stereotype of a business man. The man commanded the driver of the blue truck in a brusque way to open it. The driver of the black car came out and opened the back door where a middle aged brown haired woman emerged: slim, tall and, in a few words, a feast for the eyes. After an appraising glance on the house she went to the man, who obviously was her husband, and talked to him. That must be the new neighbors, Nick thought. He just wanted to leave his protected observation point as another person came out of the black car, it was a girl, a beautiful girl, so beautiful he had never seen before. She was tall and her long blond hair waved through the wind. Her skin was white like snow; her eyes were shining like stars. Her smile captivated him. She wore a flowered colorful dress. Simply put, she looked like a fairy. He thought she was the only child because he could not see brothers or sisters, only her and her parents. Nick observed her closely. She was quiet and she was listening to her dad because she did all the things her father ordered her to do. She didn't say anything against him. But their relationship seemed to be simply good because her father always said to her 'darling' or 'baby' or something else. Only her mother was a little bit iffy. She looked arrogant and snobbish. She was the opposite of her daughter. But they looked happy. And Nick was also happy because this gorgeous was his neighbor now. He didn't know her but he was sure that would change soon. He stopped breathing for some seconds, the most beautiful girl he had ever seen was standing just about 100 feet away.

CHAPTER 2

Some weeks passed till Nick met the mysterious girl again. She was like a good book to him, just irresistible. A few times he saw her parents running out of the house but he could never take a look at her.

It was hot, stuffy and there were a lot of people in Mr. Bence's library, a little too hot, Nick thought. He read a book about the sights of Paris, his favorite book. Nick had vowed to himself that he would visit France if he had the possibility. The little bell above the entrance rang and a girl appeared at the door. It was her. Her long blonde hair surrounded her graceful body. Over her white dress she wore a blue blouse with white ribbons. But her green eyes didn't notice Nick. She went straight to Mr. Bence and began to talk to him.

"Hello Uncle Endric." she opened. "Good afternoon, Lily. How is your father?" Mr. Bence answered.

"He is fine but that is not the reason of my visit. I want to borrow a book about the sights of Paris, do you have one?" Lily said.

"I only own one book about Paris. Nick, the youth over there has borrowed it. Shall I ask for it?" "No need, thanks." Lily said and started to go.

"No, no, no," her uncle barred her way. "I'll do it for you."

"Why? Is something wrong with him?" Lily asked her uncle.

Uncle Endric knew Nick and what their financial situation was like because Nick had had problems to pay the dues a few times.

When Lily was leaving Endric he stopped her and said: "I don't want you to get in touch with this guy because I know my brother and his attitude toward such people. Well... I don't want you to talk to him. He is not good for you; he may influence you in a bad way. His family is poor. If you were seen with him... What do you expect your father to think about you?"

Lilly listened to her uncle and what he said about this very nice-looking guy but the affection for him grew more with these words. She did not reveal her true feelings but to calm him down she claimed that she would try to get him out of the way. But she would not do what she said although Lily was sure that uncle Endric was right with what he said about her father.

Nick had not been able to follow the conversation between the girl and Mr. Bence but as the girl went to him he quickly turned around and went on reading the chapter about the Louvre. The girl from his street approached and Nick didn't know what he could say.

"Hello, my name is Lily. Are you Nick?" The girl said.

"Yes, I am. Did you move here? I never saw you in our city," Nick asked although he already knew the answer.

"Yes, my parents and I have come here from New York after my dad got a military job as a major. We live in Elm Street two blocks away." Lily said.

"I also live there with my family." was everything Nick could answer and he didn't know what else he could ask Lily so a long silence ensued his last sentence.

"Could I have this book you are currently reading? I have also many books about Paris, I can give you one instead of this. Oh, I just love that city, I am very interested in France and when I have grown up I want to visit this beautiful, magnificent, breath-taking place." she said after a long break.

"Yes, of course, this would be great and it is also my biggest dream to visit this city." Nick was overjoyed that this beautiful girl had the same interests like him. And he imagined a picture of her and him walking hand in hand through Paris looking at the sights.

"Oh, I forgot, I have to be at home in fifteen minutes, and my father will be angry if I am not on time." These words dispersed Nick's thoughts.

"Here, don't forget the book!"

"Thanks, Nick, you are kind, don't forget to visit me to get the book and maybe (if my father isn't at home) we can talk a little bit about Paris and ourselves in my room." Lily said.

"Okay, I won't forget it, that would be great. Thank you and good bye." Nick answered.

When Endric Bence saw the teenagers talking to each other in the library he wanted to admonish Lily.

Nick was absorbed in thoughts about Lily. Her perfect skin, the way she walked, she was like an angel. He didn't notice that Endric Bence approached him.

"Out of my library!" he shouted and seized Nick's neck. He dragged him through the whole library and threw him out.

CHAPTER 3

A few weeks passed, and Nick was always thinking about the new wonderful girl. He was very busy helping his parents and especially his mother, because his father was sick. One day he went with her to town to sell a gold chain she had always wanted to keep. But she needed the money now more than ever. "Your father can only get better if we buy the best medicine for him", she told Nick and his sister. Nick's father had heart desease and it was getting worse with the years.

Nick and his mother were on a dusty old bus to go to the city, which took them almost two hours. He always liked to go to the city because of all the different types of people and shops. They arrived at Senor Mierda's shop, who was buying almost everything. He was not a real jeweler but he had a lot of money, and was famous for his gold jewelry collection. Two years ago Senor Mierda had come from Mexico, and Nick's mother often sold things to him. "Hola!" he shouted when the middle-aged lady and her son came into his shop. Ten minutes later they walked out again with depressed faces and a hundred dollars in cash. Nick's Mum had been expecting at least the tenfold. After a short visit to the pharmacy they went back home and didn't talk to each other during the whole journey.

Back home he saw a little note beside the door which said "Hey, it's Lily, meet me at my house." He was happy to hear from her and immediately went to her house and rang the doorbell. A few seconds passed until Lily opened the door. Her long blonde hair was braided and she wore a red dress. He went upstairs to her big room. It was a very fantastic house with big clean windows, a floor with white marble tiles. In her room was this special fragrance. Nick felt happy when he inhaled this amazing scent. You could not compare her room with his. It was big and well-lit and everything was white. A white desk, a white bed and also a white cupboard. During the next three hours they discussed their lives and their wish to live in France, especially in Paris. They lost all feeling for the time and too soon it was late in the afternoon. Suddenly a loud noise broke the silence. They were interrupted by Mr. Bence and Lily's father who were coming back from their hunting tour. Lily became very quiet when she heard the sounds downstairs.

"My dad just came." she whispered.

"Is that a problem?" Nick asked a bit frightened.

"Yes I think so, he wouldn't want us to be friends. He hates people who don't have much money," Lily said and became quieter and quieter.

"But why, this is no real reason to hate somebody."

"I know but…" Lily stopped. "I don't care about if you have much or no money, I am interested in you and not in money. I don't need a man who has much money, I need a man who has much love for me. And I promise that this is the truth."

But..why, Lily...?" Nick tried to ask, until Lily took his hand and looked and said: "Believe me, Nick - I am serious. This is just my father's problem and not mine. I often said this, but he can't accept it. He will never change his mind, but as I told you - I don't care about it."

"I am so happy to know a girl like you," Nick said. "And I am happy to know a boy like you!" Lily whispered.

Heavy steps sounded through the door. Lily's father came up-stairs to check whether everything was alright with his daughter. A loud knock at the door frightened them. The big bull of a father came in and paused for a second.

"He is an evil parasite, throw him out of my house!" he shouted and jumped over Lily's bed. But Nick was faster, he ran around the bed, through the door and downstairs. In front of him was the unfriendly Endric with two dead rabbits over his shoulder. He opened his eyes wide and wanted to say something but Nick just jumped through the door.

CHAPTER 4

Two days later Nick was on the way to the park where Lily and he wanted to meet on the bridge. He was insecure about telling her his feelings. He became nervous when he saw her standing on the bridge. She did not see him because she had turned her back to him. Her long blonde hair looked beautiful. When she turned around she was smiling at him. He smiled back at her but he didn't feel like smiling because he was afraid of her reaction. He never had had such a feeling for a girl. He didn't know how to reveal his feelings for Lily. Lily wasn't like the girls he had known before. He had a lot of conversations and flirts with girls, but he was never speechless. He could feel his heart in his chest, how it was beating.

He tried to get into her mind, to find out what she could feel for him. He didn't want to be disappointed. Nick absolutely wanted that Lily had the same feelings like him. When he arrived at the place where Lily was standing, he looked into her eyes and took her hands. He could feel her soft skin and he would have loved to huddle her hands against his face to feel her touching him. They were very close to each other so that Nick was able to smell her. He bent down a little bit and kissed her softly. In this moment his fears flew away. He noticed a sense of release. Both of them realized in this situation that they loved each other. They didn't have to speak it out in words.

What they did not notice was that Endric Bence was only a few yards away on his way home from the library. He had just wanted to call out for Lily, when he saw Nick and stepped behind a bush. He saw it all and decided right away to tell Lily's father.

Someone knocked hard on the door and hastily kept ringing the bell. Lily went to the door very fast to open it. Lily opened the door and saw her uncle Endric. He looked very angry.

He asked: "Is your father at home?"

She said: "Yes, why? Is everything alright?"

He didn't answer the question and went directly to his brother. She followed him into the living-room.

The uncle said to his brother: "Your daughter kissed a boy this afternoon on the bridge in the park."

Lily's father asked: "Are you sure that the girl on the bridge was Lily?"

Endric answered: "Yes, I am really sure that it was her."

Lily's father couldn't believe him and told him that Lily wouldn't do things like that, otherwise she would tell him that she had a boyfriend. With hard steps he went to Lily and asked her if she had a boyfriend as his brother had told him. She asked herself if she had better tell the truth.

She finally whispered: "Yes."

The father shouted: "What did you say?"

Lily's hands were shaking and she looked at the carpet to avoid looking at her father's eyes.

Bravely she repeated loudly: "Yes, Uncle Endric is right."

The whole room was silent for a second. A second which seemed to last forever. "How shall I explain," Lily's father started as he went up and down in the room. "I cannot accept my intelligent, educated and sophisticated daughter to be in company with a poor and uncivilized kid from the street!" His voice was trembling and he turned around again.

Lily thought he became bigger and bigger and his mustache was vibrating.

"Why do you think we went here? So you become pregnant from a little ferret called Nick? No, I wanted to get you away from these apes who call themselves civilized humans and I will not accept this relationship. You will marry a decent rich man who is the son of one of my most important business partners." Lily's father shouted.

"But I love him," Lily answered nearly crying. Suddenly she felt a pain on her face, her father had slapped her so hard that she fell to the floor. She saw that she had disappointed him, but she couldn't tell him, that she would meet Nick again. He wouldn't understand it. Lily's father was a man, who had no interest in feelings. He searched for a man with money and a good reputation for his daughter.

But Lily didn't care about this. She loved Nick because of his character, the way they talked to each other for hours and she loved it, when he looked at her with his beautiful brown eyes as if she was the only girl in the world. Their favorite place to meet was the bridge. Under the bridge was a slowly flowing river which gave this place a really calm atmosphere. The picture was rounded off with wonderful smelling purple colored tulips, growing everywhere around the bridge. It was the only place where they could be alone, far away from their families and the corresponding problems. In this summer they met there every day. They were lying on the grass, eating ice cream, feeding the ducks and reading to each other from books. Somehow this place also gave them hope. Hope that one day they could fulfill their dream of Paris!

If she told all this to her father he would laugh at her and he would throw her out of the house. Or perhaps he would do something bad to Nick. Lily was afraid of her father. That was the reason why she didn't tell him anything. He was so different from Lily, but she felt that she deserved what her father had done to her. She thought she'd better obey to her father.

CHAPTER 5

'After I met Lily the first time I always thought about the moment I had to decide whether to go to war or not. Here is my endless love for Lily and the desire for her and but then again my wish to act as a proud American, to fight and defeat the enemies, so that I can come back as a war hero. But is that possible? Is it possible to survive? I am thinking about the pride of my family and the pleasure of Lily and I know I want both! At the moment I have nothing more delicious than my big love for Lily. Will that suffer? And what will my father say if I tell him?' Nick was on the way to the hospital to visit his father. He wanted to tell him something important about his future. Nick was sitting in the back seat of a cab. He didn't know how to tell his father about this.

Nick rehearsed loudly enough so the cab driver could also hear it: "Dad, I'm sorry but, no, no, no, I can't talk like this."

Suddenly he heard a laugh. Then he noticed that it was the driver who was looking into the rearview mirror and said: "My boy, don't worry, your father will forgive you. When I was your age I also made mistakes, don't worry."

Then Nick looked out and said: "You don't know the trouble I'm in." But he talked so quietly that the driver couldn't hear him. They arrived at the hospital and Nick paid and ran inside to look for the room where his father was. Finally he found the room and before he knocked he went through in his mind what and how he wanted to tell his father.

A few minutes later Nick's hands trembled as he held the hand of his sick father. He had tears in his eyes and was very sad because he knew that his father did not have very much time left.

He looked his father into the blood-shot eyes and felt the trembling of his pale body. Nick pulled together all his strength to prepare his father for his decision. He just did not know how to begin and wished Lily were at his side. She would know best how he could tell his father. He had not told her of his plan because he did not want to hurt her.

He sat in silence for a long time, looking down at his father, and finally began to speak softly: "Listen to me, father... I have a dream."

For the first time something moved in his father's face, who began to speak with difficulty: "I am listening, son."

"The stories you told me about the time when you were at war have always fascinated me. Since then, I have been dreaming to go to war just like you did. I want you to have a reason to be proud of me, father!"

"You always make me proud, you always made me happy. You have always been a good son." his father said, smiling gently. "Why have you never told me before? You should make your dreams come true, my boy, as long as you have the time."

Completely surprised by his father's reaction and relieved to have received his approval, he burst into tears and hugged his father, careful like a mother with a newborn not to hurt the fragile body. His father could not control his emotion either and started to cry as well.

Suddenly Nick remembered a day on a playground in his neighborhood, years ago when he was eight. The sunshine on his face felt the same like on the day when he had been there with his father and his young sister. At that moment Nick felt that he was able to hear the soft voice of his father right now how he had asked him whether he wanted an ice cream. Always when Nick had been together with his father he had felt that he was complete because James had given him the feeling that he was the best son ever. Nick could only remember his father as a very nice man who took care of his children when he was at home. Nick wasn't able to spend much time with his father so the times when they were together had been very precious. James' biggest wish had been to become a major in the army so he had used most of his time to reach this goal and to learn enough – he had wanted more money to ensure a good life for his family. Nick remembered clearly how his father had promised every day to come home early to eat dinner with the family but every day he had waited in vain because his father had never kept this promise.

Some days later Nick's father died of a heart attack. In spite of the sadness deep inside him Nick felt happy that his father had blessed his dreams. With the approval of his father he felt comfortable about going to war.

After thinking about his feelings for Lily, he remembered their last minutes together. They had been standing on the bridge talking about some ideas for a future when they could live together and be happy. First they had thought how they could convince Lily's parents to accept that they wanted to have a future together. After some bad ideas they had noticed that there was no way. They had been frustrated and kept quiet while they had been looking at the ground. Nick suddenly had had an idea.

He had shouted: "We don't have to convince them, we can go our own way"!

She had asked: "How do you think this could work"?

"We don't really need much money to be happy. I think love is enough. We could run away and have a little apartment in a big city. I would work as a mechanic and you could study. And if the money lasts for an apartment and enough to eat it will be enough".

Lily had looked very afraid and shocked. She hadn't known what he had wanted to hear from her. But she couldn't lie. She had looked at him, kissed him for the last time and had walked away.

In the winter of 1940 Nick went to war in France. The distance was very hard on her. She had cried at the farewell but she had accepted it. "I promise, I will see you again," had been his last words at the final parting.

CHAPTER 6

Nick was in his barrack for a short hour off-duty, musing about the next steps: 'Today it is June 5th, 1944. In five hours "Operation Neptune" will turn into its final phase and I am only lying and thinking. Fear? No! Lots of my comrades are happy to fight against the Germans for their country but I think it will be a massacre on the beach of Omaha in Normandy, France. Of course I also think about my mother. Where is she now at this moment ? What is she doing and how is she? I only hope she is fine. I am afraid of never seeing her again, that something happens to her while I am here. Now while I am ready to die for the U.S.A.

But what bothers me the most is Lily. I love her so much and miss her so hard. Does she feel the same? Does she still love me or has she found somebody new? I don't know. I couldn't handle it if I came back and she wasn't my girl anymore. Thinking of her gives me so much and I guess if it wouldn't be for her I couldn't get through the days here.'

'Five days have passed since the beginning of the operation and we are hopelessly stuck and hungry in the dig protect. Our sergeant says that we have to sleep a little bit, to be fit for the next days. When I am sleeping, I always dream about the battle on Omaha beach. It was a rainy day and we were in the boats in direction of the beach. The average age of the soldiers was 20. We were the 29th Division of the U.S Army and unfortunately the first platoon landing on the beach. Most of the soldiers weren't trained well. Some were afraid and others were seasick.

The boatman yelled: "The last 30 seconds, soldiers - God be with you!"

When the boats arrived at the beach, bombs exploded everywhere, and machine-guns fired. The door of our boat opened and hundreds of bullets crashed into the bodies of the soldiers. I only saw falling soldiers and I crouched and went forward to a hollow which had been created by a bomb. I looked at the beach and saw dead soldiers, soldiers without legs and arms, it was terrible. For the time being I was still sitting in the hollow and saw more and more boats with soldiers, they arrived at the beach. Only after eight and a half hours we could advance to the checkpoint beta and overrun the enemy troops. We occupied the beach, later I heard that 2.000 soldiers had died at the first landing on the beach. That was nine out of ten who had been in the attacking wave. For one second I was really happy to be alive, but then I thought of the families of the dead soldiers, of their children and began to cry. It was the first time that I cried in the war, but not because of myself, but because of all the friendly comrades who had fallen that day. Lost between the sea and the German troop points. Every second there can be an attack of the enemies now and we are only waiting here for commands.'

CHAPTER 7

Dear Nick,

How are you? I hope you are fine. I miss you very much and the time without you is very hard. I miss your voice which makes me so happy, I miss your smell, I miss everything. Every night before sleeping I imagine how life would be if you came back now. When I finally can hug you and together we can fulfill our dream to visit Paris.

By the way I have read the book "Sights of Paris" completely and it is fascinating. I remember the first time we met in uncle Endric's library. I was very shy and you were very nervous. I never told you that my uncle had seen us on the bridge where we kissed and he told my father about our relationship. He slapped me and locked me up in my room. He could never understand our love. Now he is trying to marry me to a stranger, so the only way is to run away.

I am worried about the future, because of all the trouble I have to fight here. Our relationship is fading away with every day you are not near me. I know my trouble is not similar to yours but I need you now more than ever in this hard time! Please come back and hold me and protect me from the troublemaker, who I called dad in my childhood. It's like fog in my head, I can't live without you and I will never accept to get married to that stupid other guy. Please, please come back!

Lily

Lily's father had a talk with his wife about the planning of the wedding. They decided to tell Lily Nick was dead to convince her of the marriage.

"Are you sure you want to lie to Lily?" Lily's mother asked her husband.

"Nick isn't the one for Lily! You know that! He has no good reputation, no money, nothing! She must get married to John!" her husband answered.

Endric Bence nodded to his brother.

"I'm not sure, if that is the best way..." she said with a quizzical expression.

"Nobody has asked you! It's my decision and she will get married to John, Nick is 'dead'... do you understand me?" he said loudly to his wife.

"Well if you think that is the best solution, then go and tell her that Nick is dead!" she said.

"Yes, let that be my concern.", he grumbled and asked his brother to go upstairs and tell Lily that he would like to have a serious conversation with her.

Lily had been staring out of the window for hours lost in thoughts about Nick. Suddenly she was interrupted by her uncle, who came into her room. He said that her father was waiting in the kitchen in order to talk about something very important. Without any word Lily went downstairs to the kitchen to hear what her father had to say.

Her father was busy slicing some vegetables but he had noticed Lily's steps. He asked her to set the table for dinner but Lily's attention was on the necklace Nick had given her as a farewell gift. It was a golden chain with a pyramid and inside was an eye.

"I will always be at your side", he had said as he had given her the jewelry.

Again she was awakened from her dream by her father's voice.

"Sit down, we have to talk", he said.

"It's about Nick, honey, I am very sad but he was killed in an airstrike yesterday".

Although it was as if a hurricane was racing through her heart she could not even move a finger. She felt how the pain deadened her whole body from head to toe. She was alone from now on and the only thing in her mind was that Nick would never return to her.

Then she collapsed and broke down in the arms of her father. That night Lily dreamt of Nick in a meadow where he was lying with a book in his hands - their favorite book about Paris. The setting sun shone directly on his perfect face. In this light he looked prettier than ever so she approached him gently not to disturb him while he was reading.

In her dream she was able to see that a butterfly with yellow wings was flying over Nick and sat itself on the book. With a smile Lily awoke and became immediately aware of the fact that she was never going to see him again while he was reading. Everything, their dreams, their plans, her best friend, her big love was gone. She cried herself back to sleep while her hands held on tightly to her necklace.

Nick was lying on his bed with a beautiful photo of Lily and talked to the photo:

'I know the distance is a factor, but I stretch as far as I can in my mind as often as I can. My goal is to reach your hands any day now. Please don't blame me for trying to push you when we saw each other for the last time. I am having a hard time as it is, because I miss your love. When I come back, don't act like you don't know me, it is still me, I never changed. I'll be there one time. And even though you are far away now, you are still here somehow and I need you to know I miss you. I miss your smile and I still shed some tears here every once in a while because I still miss you so badly.'

CHAPTER 8

After Lily had told her father that she and Nick were in a relationship, Lily's father had slapped and imprisoned her in the house. Then he had told her Nick was dead. He had looked for someone who fitted her perfectly from his point of view and found one. It was the son of an old friend of his. His name was John. He was large, powerful and he was able to support Lily in financial affairs. So Lily's father decided that Lily and John had to get married. Both family members, including John agreed with the marriage, except Lily. She didn't know John very well and the most important fact was that she loved Nick and wanted to marry only him. Even though she knew that this was never going to happen, because he would not come back, so Lily was on her own. She had to care for herself.

Lily was sitting in her room when her father entered and saw her crying.

"Why are you crying? This should be the best day of your live." her father said.

"You know that I can't love John, dad, I have to get married to a man whom I don't love, it is the worst day of my life. I want to be dead!" Lily yelled into her father's face.

He grabbed her arm and pulled at her. Lily was shocked and covered her face with her hands. Tears ran over her face.

Her father looked at her with a look she had never seen before. It was a mix of despair and anger.

"You have to do what I think is best for you Lily."

"Dad, please don't do this to me, I will never be happy and you know that."

"The time will heal your wounds and you will forget Nick."

"No", Lily yelled, "I will never forget him, I swear that I will never love someone else!"

Her father grabbed her arm again. Lily did not dare to look at her father's face.

"You have to marry John, whether you love him or not. Nick is dead and will never come back again so forget him, Lily."

Her father left the room and Lily fell to her knees and began to cry. She cried and cried desperately for Nick but then she realized that Nick could not hear her and that he would never come back like her father had said. She was completely power-less and felt broken: "Oh God, will that be my fate?"

The ceremony took place at St. Michael's Church. Almost the whole town was present, because Lily's father was a wealthy, but also highly estimated businessman whom no one wanted as an enemy. They were all dressed up, the men wore black tuxedos, the ladies long, some of them short evening dresses. Each family or each couple were trying to be at their best. But even if Lily's heart was broken, on the outsight she looked perfect, her make-up was as it had to be, and her hair as well. She was a gorgeous bride and beyond competition the most beautiful girl in town.

Lily cried during the whole ceremony while all the guests thought that she was happy but she wasn't happy at all.

Her mother came and asked her: "Why are you crying, my little girl? This must be the happiest day in your life?"

"Mom, I don't love him. I love Nick."

Lily's mother's eyes became sad as she was beginning to think about herself. 'I feel sorry for her but... No, that must be right', she thought, 'life isn't a fairy tale and we all have to know the place we belong to. Even if she does not love him I am sure that it is the duty of every woman to act like a good, obedient wife and mother. Because it's the best for everyone.'

"Lily, I don't want to hear anything about Nick anymore! You are John's wife and you must forget Nick."

"But Mom, ..."

"Stop it! Now smile and be proud of your good husband and fulfill your obligations as a wife this night and for rest of your life!"

The wedding was celebrated in a grand ballroom. Everyone danced and wished the new couple the best. Late in the evening, Lily and John went to John's home. For the first time Lily saw her future home. As she beheld the estate, her thoughts became melancholic musing about her situation.

'John's house is wonderful; the golden lamps overhead are the most beautiful lamps I have ever seen before. The whole house is furnished expensively and glamorously. John shows me every room in the house. The house has six bedrooms, four bathrooms and two living rooms. The garden that surrounds the estate is so big that it could even be compared to a park. Although I am used to this lifestyle and these people and what they possess it is overwhelming for me to see this big beautiful house.'

John and Lily went to the last bedroom of the house. John smiled at Lily and softly touched her cheek. John whispered that she was the most beautiful girl he had ever met. He kissed her neck and started to open her dress. Tears were running down her face.

"Lily, don't be scared, I will be a good husband."

"John, I can't ..."

"Lily, from now on you are my wife and you have to behave like one."

So Lily did what she had to do and for the first time had sex with her husband, whom she did not really love and know! It was the worst night in her life and Lily felt dirty, used, and unloved. She had imagined her first time very differently. Instead of John it should have been Nick who deflowered her and there should have been candles and rose petals and in the background beautiful, hot, romantic music should have been played.

CHAPTER 9

The whole situation broke Lily physically and mentally. Her life felt like a bad movie, every day the same procedures: get ready, have breakfast, relax, eat lunch, read, spend time with the family, have dinner and once in a while fulfill the marital duties with her husband John. But it was all bloody pretenses and every day her parents came over to join them for hours.

Even when they ate together at the table they never had the familiar atmosphere. Why should they? Not one of the family members was willing to cook.

Once it happened that her mother fired the cook, because she didn't like the meal and she wanted everything to be perfect at dinner. She was 'Mrs. Perfect'. Lily was annoyed and angry because of her mother. 'How could she be so heartless and not think about the people she fires?' Lily asked herself. She liked to assist in the kitchen and to help preparing the meal. This afternoon Lily's mother tried to make the dinner, but it was far from being delicious. Then John found a new cook. She was not as intelligent as the one before. The new cook was boring so Lily decided to talk to the housecleaner and help her to banish the boredom. She could not stand it anymore to stay in a room with the whole family especially with her father, who in her eyes had become the most terrible person in the world besides her mother's control addiction.

The sincere, loving and kind nature of John helped her to stand the whole situation, although he also sometimes showed a negative side of his character. That happened one morning.

Lily got up early. She got ready and went down to the kitchen to get herself a glass of water. So she went into the dining room and suddenly saw a perfectly decorated and prepared breakfast table, including tasteful delicacies like ham, bacon, eggs and homemade jam. She still looked fascinated at the table as John appeared and smiled brightly at her.

"Good morning, darling, how did you sleep and did you have sweet dreams?"

Regarding her bad situation because she was married to John, it wasn't possible for her to be happy about John's morning present, she could only answer "Yes" in a rather cold way. They sat down without talking to each other, but John always tried to start a conversation.

"Would you like a cup of tea, darling?"

"No, thank you, John."

"What are you going to do after breakfast? I know a nice place to walk."

"No, thank you, I'd rather read my book today."

John felt Lily's cold behavior and started to get a little bit angry. He sat down beside Lily, took her hand and started to play with her fingers, but Lily didn't like this and pulled her hand away.

"Lily, is everything alright with you?"

"What do you mean by this?"

He took her arm and said: "You have been denying all my efforts for days now!"

Lily only answered: "Really?" in a cold way.

"Yes, really!" John said with an aggressive voice. "Seriously… do you think you are something special? I could have any women I want! You should better be thankful for having such a great husband as me."

A moment of silence filled the room but suddenly with a really quiet voice Lily said: "Thankful? For what?"

John lifted his arm and wanted to hit her in her face, but right before he hit her, he stopped and his arm went down and he walked away. Lily had never seen a person with such two different kinds of behavior before. That wasn't the first and not the last time that John became that aggressive. Day by day he became angrier and more violent.

CHAPTER 10

'There were lots of counterattacks of the Germans to get the beach back, but we blocked all of them and defended the beach. All divisions and also the 29th were moved to the centre of France. We got some new privates to our divisions. Every single one of them was so young and innocent. Paris was our main target to get. From 19th August until 25th August we fought for Paris and finally got in. I have almost adapted to the war by now. The dead and injured, everything is my daily life now.

I remember and miss the life with Lily. I miss laughing, talking, hanging around with her, hugging her and especially kissing her sweet lips, even if we had to hide for that. And for this I am here, here in this hell - this isn't and shouldn't be my life. I really want to go back to Lily and keep the most important promise to myself, but ... Lily is so far away! Sometimes I ask myself, what it would be like if things had been different. Maybe I would be together with her. We would lie in the sun and laugh together. I must trust her. I cannot trust anyone but Lilly. I want to be the first and the last one who is loved by Lily. We were supposed to come together. Lily is waiting for me. When I'm with her I shall hold her hand and give her all the hours back I didn't spend with her. I want her right now and always. And I know Lily is thinking like me. She is sitting in her room, looking out of the window and waits to be together with me.

Sometimes I think if I give up, it's over. But if I don't, the day will come when I'll be glad I didn't give up. Lily is waiting and the day will come when we will be together forever. When our two hearts are meant for each other, no distance is too far and no time is too long and no other man can break our love...

We stayed in Paris for some days. We were relaxing there. Suddenly our commanders came in and yelled: "Come on boys, it is beginning again. Do you want to live forever?" Our next stop was Belgium.

I personally think that the resistance of the Germans is breaking down, because there are fewer battles for villages or cities now…

It's May 8th 1945. I can't hear the guns anymore, the war is finally over. We are going back to our camps. It is very dark, we cannot see all the dead bodies on the street but the smell of them is everywhere in the air. I can't believe that so many of our soldiers died. I am very proud of them and at the same time I am happy that the war is over and I can finally go back home to Lily and my family. It's very strange that Lily didn't answer my letters. I hope everything is fine.'

CHAPTER 11

When Nick came back from war he expected everything to be the same. But everything had changed. He arrived at home hoping he could hold his mother in his arms again. What he didn't know was that his mother wasn't there.

While he was standing there confused about his mother's absence he saw the overfilled mailbox. He was wondering why there were all these letters in it and why nobody had emptied the mailbox. He opened it and found all the letters he had written to his mother which had not been answered the weeks before he came back.

"You are her son, right?" someone asked, whose voice Nick had never heard before.

Nick turned around and saw a man who reminded him of his father. The way he stood there looking into Nick's eyes was like his father had always used to do.

"I am." Nick answered.

The stranger told Nick about his mother's disease and that she had been taken to the hospital a few weeks before.

"She has...cancer?"

"I'm sorry, but yes."

The stranger said he had moved to their street last summer and got to know his mother when Nick had still been in the war. They had become good friends the stranger told Nick.

He felt that he had to see his mother in the hospital and to be there for her after the long time they hadn't seen each other. He felt bad because he hadn't been there when she had needed him most. He had gone to war to make his parents proud of him, but now he felt like he had made the biggest mistake in his life.

His neighbor took him to the hospital. At the information desk Nick asked for his mother.

"Floor 3, room 248." the bored woman answered.

He said: "Thank you." and went to the room where his sick mother was lying.

His mother was sleeping when he came in. Nick slowly closed the door because he didn't want to wake her up. But she woke up and her look went to the door and for a moment the room was filled with total silence.

"Hi Mum." Nicks Mother couldn't control her emotions and started to cry. But at the same moment she had to smile and laugh. She tried to get up and grab her son to give him a strong and big hug.

"Oh, Nick! You are just crazy! You are just so crazy surprising me here like this. I missed you so much!"

Nick seemed to be overwhelmed by the situation, too, and was not able to say something. He just held his mother in his arms and had a big smile on his face.

"How are you my son? Is everything all right with you? I'm so happy to see you."

"I'm fine. I'm just worried about you."

He sat down on the chair next to the bed his mother was lying in.

He took her hand and held it. Again she tried to get up a bit to hug her son but she wasn't able to.

"Lay down." Nick said.

"I'm so glad to see you." his mother answered while she smiled at him.

"I'm fine. I'm just worried about you."

"You don't need to. Everything will be fine."

Nick knew that she wasn't really sure about it when he looked into his mothers eyes. He saw fear in her eyes but obviously she didn't want to talk about it.

"Your sister has gone." Nick's mother said.

"What do you mean by she has gone?" Nick asked.

"As I told you, Nick. She has gone to New York with her husband. I told her she was too young, but she didn't care. She is now working in a hotel. She wanted to become a famous journalist. I told her."

"Why isn't she here? Here with you?"

"Oh, Nick... Can't you understand? She was so young when your father died. I don't want her to be in the same situation again. I think she couldn't handle it." she explained to him.

"She needs to know, Mom!" Nick replied. "What if she finds out? What are you going to tell her? And if she doesn't... What are you going to tell her if it gets worse?"

"I'll decide when the time comes. For now it's not necessary to bother her."

"But you can't go through this on your own." Nick said.

"Yes, I can... I need to." his mother contradicted.

"No, you don't need to. I am here for you and she also will but first you need to tell her. If you don't tell her I will. I mean it!"

"No! Nick, please don't do that. I beg you. I really don't want her to know about it until it's definitely necessary." she requested.

On the one hand Nick understood why his mother didn't want to tell his sister. She wanted to protect her. But on the other hand Nick believed that his sister should know about it and that his mother needed her support.

"Okay. But promise me that you'll tell her if it gets worse." Nick required.

"I promise." she replied. They said nothing to each other for a while.

"And how do you feel with it?" she asked Nick.

"What with?"

"With Lily's marriage, of course."

Nick felt a weird feeling welling up inside him. Like a mix of angriness, sadness and confusion. When his mother saw the way Nick looked at her she knew that he had not known about it.

"I'm sorry. I thought you knew." she said surprised.

Nick didn't know what to say. Right then he could only think that this day couldn't get any worse.

After a few minutes he said: "I need to talk to Lily."

She nodded and said he should go now to talk to her. Nick asked if she was sure because he didn't want her to be alone.

"The sooner the better." she said and smiled.

"Okay," Nick said, "but I will be back as soon as possible."

"Alright, see you then."

"Bye." Nick said and quickly went out of the room.

CHAPTER 12

Only a little while later he stood in front of Lily's house. He was nervous. When he wanted to ring the doorbell, he didn't find the name he was searching for. He was surprised, but still wanted to ring the door bell. A little girl opened the door. She was about four years old. Nick was shocked.

"Is your mom at home?" he asked.

The girl called for her mother and the young woman who now approached the door wasn't Lily. He took a deep breath and was glad. The young lady looked at him and asked him who he was and what he wanted. Nick told her, that he lived next to her house and that he was searching for a 'Lily'. The woman said with a sad smile that she didn't know anything about the people, who had lived in the house before her. Nick looked scared; a thousand things were running through his head. Suddenly he had an idea. Quickly he said: "Thank you, madam."

Nick ran as fast as he could to the library, where he got a curious look from Mr. Bence.

"Where is she?" Nick demanded from Mr. Bence.

"Where is who?" he answered.

"Where is LILY?" Nick began to get angry.

Mr. Bence looked scared and held his hands against his face. "Please, sir. I don't know!"

"You know where she is! Tell me!" Nick was really angry now. Very slowly and badly he hissed: "Tell me ...now!"

"Ok, Sir. She moved away! She married a very polite man and they are happy, so leave them alone!"

Nick couldn't say anything. His face turned white. He couldn't breathe anymore. He screamed and threw a lot of books from the table to the floor.

"The address! Give it to me!"

Mr. Bence was so scared, he took a piece of paper and wrote down Lily's new address without a further word. He handed it to him and Nick grabbed it and ran out of the library. He looked at it and saw that the street where Lily lived was just one mile from the library. He started to run. He wanted to see her. He wanted to talk to her. He couldn't believe what she had done to him.

CHAPTER 13

After a while, he stood in front of the big house and looked at all the beautiful flowers in the garden. He went straight to the door. With a strange feeling, he stood in front of the door and began to ring.

Nick heard footsteps which became louder and louder and his heart began to run faster and faster. Suddenly he heard a female voice saying: "Who is this?"

He was sure that it was Lily's voice and his heart beat even faster than before and he didn't know what to answer. His thoughts went crazy, as they had always done in Lily's presence. Then Lily opened the door. At first Nick looked into her eyes which brought back all the beautiful memories. Lily was standing in front of him and also gazed into Nick's eyes. No one was speaking. He took the chance to look at Lily in detail.

'Short hair, looking exhausted and with dark circles under the eyes, and a thin body that looks fragile, this woman has nothing in common with my Lily of the old days but for me this girl is the most beautiful woman in the world. Damn, Nick, why do you still have doubts about her? Look into her eyes, the depth of the sea is reflected in them like in the past. No, no this can't be. No matter how many years have passed I know that a person cannot change its whole personality, this is simply impossible. This woman is not Lily! Her uncle must have lied to me! But then, why do I feel so attracted to this woman? I don't know what is going on with me...'

The woman began to speak, and a quiet, slightly hoarse but still gentle voice took Nick back into his youth. Now he could be sure, without any doubts. The woman who stood in front of him was his Lily! She had short blond hair and her green eyes opened wide, when she saw the person, who was standing there in front of her.

Within split seconds Lily had recognized Nick and was astounded. 'These eyes... could it be? Who is this man? He looks like... no it cannot be, do we have a new postman? Hmm... these eyes... these big brown eyes... why are they so familiar? No... it is him... My one and only love... Nick! Oh my goodness, I can't believe it, is it really him? Is that just a dream? After all the great things we did - He has changed so much. His eyes are telling me he missed me, his shoulders are so strong, the scars on his arms. Is that the boy I really loved, is that just a dream? After all these years, I've completely forgotten him, this cannot be true and if it is him, what is going to happen to us? What had happened to my father, how could he look me in my eyes, after these lies? I don't know, what I shall do, I am so confused. This only can be a dream. Does he know, that I thought that he was dead?'

"Oh my God, Nick! What are you doing here, I thought you were dead!" She came out and closed the door behind her.

Nick was confused. "Dead? Who told you that? I always said, I'll come back to you, Lily!"

Lily didn't know what to say. Instead she fell into his arms, she began to cry and to laugh at the same time. She was so happy to see him. Nick didn't know how long they were holding each other, but it felt so good.

Then he pushed her away softly and asked her: "You're married?"

Lily looked at the ground. "It wasn't my decision... My parents told me you were dead. They searched for a 'good' man for me. I don't love him, Nick! Everyday I was waiting for you. Everyday I hoped you would stand in front of me. Every day I talked to God ..."

Nick looked at her, took her hand and whispered in her ear: "Come! We'll go away! We'll leave them all here and just live our life, together!"

Lily looked into his brown eyes and smiled and said: "Yes!"

Nick smiled back, kissed her and whispered: "A week from today at five in the morning I will stand here."

She looked so happy and kissed him. "But we'll meet tomorrow, too! See you tomorrow, Nick!" she said with a smile and went inside. Nick smiled like the sun, turned around and suddenly thought of his mother again.

CHAPTER 14

A day before Nick and Lily had planned to disappear, Nick wanted to visit his mother for a final time but her condition had turned to the worse. He did not know what to do. He felt that he couldn't abandon his mother because she needed his help. He was thinking all night about it and decided he had to stay by her side.

The next morning he and Lily met in the park. Nick took all his courage and confessed his decision to Lily: "Lily .. I would love to go away with you, but I can't leave my mother behind. She is in the hospital because of her cancer. I don't know how long she will make it."

Lily said: "Oh my God, I am so sorry! Why are you not with her? Come Nick, I will go with you."

After two hours, they both reached the hospital. Nick went to the information desk. The woman behind the desk smiled and nodded at Nick. Lily took Nick's hand and they went to the stairs. Before they reached the stairs a man with a white coat, dark hair and big glasses ran towards them. It was Doctor Neil. Nick knew him because he was his mother's doctor.

"Hello, Doctor Neil! How are you?" Nick asked. "Hello Nick, I must talk to you. Please sit down."

Nick looked worried at Lily. Lily softly pressed Nick's hand. He sat down in a black chair.

"Nick..., I'm sorry to tell you this. Your mother died this morning at 6 am. We did everything we could but it was not enough. Her last words were: Nick is the best son that I ever could have had. She died with a smile on her face. Nick, we are sorry." the doctor said consolatory. "Maybe she is now in a better place."

Nick was quiet and looked at Lily and then at the doctor and then again at Lily. He had tears in his eyes. Lily took him in her arms. The doctor mumbled something like he would leave them alone. Now Nick cried and sobbed loudly. Lily asked him, if he wanted to go outside. Nick didn't answer, felt he needed air and went outside. Lily ran after him. She reached him at the bench: "Nick I'm so..."

"Please, Lily, don't talk about it. Please..." Nick interrupted her. They both said nothing for a few minutes. "Lily..? Please let's go to France." Nick said quietly.

"Nick, I also have to tell you something. When I'm honest, I also have thought about it all last night, because I wasn't sure myself whether it was the right decision to leave with you."

"Why? I thought that you wanted to begin a new life with me."

"Yes, but I can't disappoint my family and John would find us anyway."

"Are you saying that you prefer to stay with John rather than with me?"

"Nick I will always love you and you know that better than myself. But it was a mistake that I married John only because my parents expected me to. Now I have to live with the consequences, we are not children anymore. Maybe I will never be in love with John or happy with him but there is no way back. John is certainly far from perfect but after all he is my husband. We both should accept that there is no future for us together, sometimes love just isn't enough, honey. Today you have lost your mother, Nick, and I don't want to lose my mother, either. If I left John for you it would just kill her. This disappointment would be too much for her. We are not alone on earth even though I wish that we were. And Nick, I know you will understand this."

Nick nodded and looked down and just said: "I know, Lily."

"Nick, you know I love you above all else, but it's not working. You have to forget me."

Nick grabbed her by her arm and replied angrily: "Do you think it's that easy to forget you and just stop loving you? You were the only good thing that kept me alive during the war."

Lily took her bag and with tears in her eyes she shouted back at Nick: "Nick, you don't understand me!"

"I know exactly what you mean!" Nick said frustrated and turned around. Lily looked at his back for a short while.

"But, I love you Nick ..." she said quietly and left him standing there.

CHAPTER 15

When Lily woke up the next morning it was very hard to get up. She tried to but she was full of pain. Then she went to the bathroom and stood in front of the washbasin. She saw her face in the mirror. Suddenly she cried and pictures of yesterday went through her mind - all that had happened the evening before. She tried to wash her face but her face felt as if it was burning. Then the telephone rang. Lily took a towel for her face and ran to pick up the phone. It was her mom.

"How are you?" she asked. Lily couldn't hold her tongue. She tried to tell her mother that she was fine, but her mother noticed the trace in her voice that betrayed her. She asked: "What happened?" Lily's mother was a bit nervous, she had already started to guess what could have happened.

Lily answered: "It's always the same. Yesterday evening he came home from work and I hadn't changed for dinner. He shouted at me and said very bad things to me, like I'm a bad wife and not useful. I cried and said to him he should be quiet and he should leave me alone, but he only laughed at me and slapped me in my face, as if I were a stupid dog, which had made a mistake. Everyday we yell at each other and have so many conflicts. There are just little things, which get him to hit me. He always searches for mistakes that I make. I can't stand this anymore. Please, mum, you must understand me and accept my opinion. It's so hard to tell you this now. He isn't normal. He is crazy! Please mum, help me! Imagine you were in my situation. What would you do? I want to tell you a secret. Please promise me you won't tell sanybody. Not dad and not uncle Endric and not JOHN! Nobody may know this, it doesn't make sense to stay here. I have a dream! My biggest wish is to go to France to start something new! To live my life and not think about the past. If I stay here, it will destroy my life, mum."

Her mom started to cry and said: "My lovely daughter, we are so sorry, what can we do now? How should we have known that he'd turn out like that? We are so sorry!"

Lily put the receiver down. She cried loudly and prayed to God to take her life. "I have lost Nick for good and my marriage is a wreck. But enough is enough." she said, "I can't wait for someone to do something, I have to take it in my own hands." Lily ran to the bridge were she had so often met Nick and thought about the past with him.

She thought about the moments in the past when she had felt happy with her parents. Those were the ones when she was woken up by her mother's voice every morning and when they all sat at the table and had breakfast together. Her father was reading the newspaper every morning while her mother was in the kitchen baking fresh bread. Lily suddenly could smell the fresh bread again. Tears got in her eyes and the first tear rolled down her right cheek. She also remembered the first meeting with Nick. The meeting which had changed her life completely. All the pain she had had to endure. The moment she had to believe that Nick - her big love - was dead. She had been so happy when they were together. Every moment with him had been like an escape for her. A flight into safety, an escape from the strict standards of her parents. With Nick she was free.

All these wonderful moments with Nick appeared in front of her eyes. There she was overwhelmed by a heat, a heat that seemed to be so familiar to her and gave her a sense of security. But the next moment she felt cold, cold because the worst day of her life came into her mind. She had to live with her parents' wishes in regard to a marriage with a man who was so strange to her. John was like a nightmare she had to go through. Lily remembered the nights when John came home drunk and aggressive and beat her. She could still feel every single stroke and she remembered all the insults he had thrown at her. All the time she had survived the torture, all the psychological pressure after he treated her badly, all these things were going through her head before the first tears of her eyes dropped to the floor. Suddenly Lily felt strange in her own body, without realizing she took her first step from the bridge. She closed her eyes and felt the ground beneath and her feet disappear. Again she felt free as in the times with Nick, the times without any worries. Lily smiled. She heard Nick's voice which called her name.

Suddenly she felt a firm pressure on her right upper arm which pulled her back a little and put her back on solid ground. She realized that Nick's voice was real. She opened her eyes and looked at Nick. She couldn't believe her eyes. Nick was really there.

"Nick, is it really you?" She stroked his cheek and held his face in her hands.

Nick grabbed her hands and asked her with a shocked look: "Lily, can you tell me what you're doing here? Do you think that your life is that worthless?!"

With a face that was full of pain she looked at Nick's face.

"No, Nick, my life is not worth anything. I'm not the person that you know anymore. My live is like a trip to hell!"

Nick gently put his hand on her cheek and turned her head so that she looked him in his eyes again. The tears now ran freely over Lily's cheeks and she tried not to look into Nicks eyes.

"Look at me, Lily, do you believe that it was easy for me to live without you? You being the only reason for me to live? That fact that you are married to another man… do you think that this was easy for me? Can't you believe that I dream every damn night of our small, wonderful family with our small house and our small garden?"

Lily looked him into his eyes.

"I can't stand this anymore. All the hope that I had, that we will come together is gone. I don't want to live anymore, Nick!"

Nick started to become louder:

"Lily, you want to leave me alone?! I can't live without you."

"Nick, listen to me!"

"NO! Lily! You listen to me! I love you! I'm also going through a really hard time but I would never be that selfish to leave you alone on this world, just to escape all the pain in my life. Don't forget I'm here and I'll be always here to take a little bit of your pain. We have to stand together!"

"Nick … I want … "

"Don't say anything, Lily! I know you are broken inside like me but you have to be strong …the last time! We will make our dream of being together come true and until then we have to support each other. We love each other and nothing is stronger than love!"

Again Lily looked into Nick's eyes. Suddenly the hope was back. She smiled and Nick hugged her really intensely. Lily felt safe and strong. With Nick, she wanted to fulfill her dream!

CHAPTER 16

In the following weeks Lily and Nick didn't meet often but when they met and were together, they forgot the world around them and everything was fine. For hours they sat in a café and laughed a lot. Nick told her stories of the war which were exciting but also sad. Very carefully she listened to his stories and was fascinated by what Nick had experienced. Every meeting with Nick was something special. They did not talk about the "typical topics" like other pairs. They talked about everything: history, politics but also about questions which made no sense. "Why is the sky blue?" or "How many species of flowers are there in the world?"

But most of the time she still spent with her husband John. John had improved, he didn't drink as much as before and he didn't treat Lily as bad as before. But one night John came to bed and told Lily: "Lily, I think we must behave like a normal wife and husband." Lily looked confused and then John came near her and tried to kiss her. He tried to plague her, but Lily did not have a chance to stand his attack. From this day on it went this way again and again.

Lily and Nick met one day in a park. She did not tell him about the terrible nights with John. But Nick observed from Lily's behavior, that something was wrong with her. Lily was absent all the time and said nothing.

Thoughts were going around in her head like a constant discussion with a second person within her: 'My love for Nick is always growing, just the thought of cutting him out of my life breaks my heart. I love my parents, I love Nick and I don't want to hurt anybody. I know that I will never be happy if I stay with John, but there is no possibility to escape. I want to be far away from here with Nick by me side. There is nobody that loves me as much as Nick does but I don't see a future for us.

I have to make a decision, shall I decide for a life with John and stay unhappy or shall I decide for Nick against my parents and John? There is so much anxiety, so many questions and no answers.

I spend days in my room and feel like I'm doing absolutely nothing. I'm constantly hoping that things will get better, but I'm also wondering if they actually ever will. And the worst part? When I'm trying to be okay with that feeling of sadness, depression pulls me back in and then I crash evern harder than before. I have to go back there to John and pretend that everything's fine. I feel devastated but I have to learn living without Nick.'

Suddenly Lily didn't feel good and her stomach started to hurt. She was heaving and Nick asked: "What's wrong? Are you ill?"

"No I'm alright... I've got to go!"

At home Lily's stomach started to hurt even more. She was lying on the bed and tried not to move, so that it was less painful. John was worried about Lily and he took care of her. Lily was surprised of John. She had never seen this caring, worried and good side of him.

"Lily,... let me drive you to Dr. Demsey! He can help you."

John and Lily drove to the doctor and Dr. Demsey came to his diagnosis. While they were waiting for the results, the nurse called Lily to the doctor.

"Dr. Demsey , tell me what's wrong with me."

"Sit down Madame. Nothing is wrong with you!"

Lily sat down on the chair.

"Congratulations, Madam! You are pregnant!"

Lily was shocked and stared into space. She stood up and walked into the waiting room. John asked her: "Did you get the results?" Lily answered with a smile on her face: "Everything is all right; it's just a simple viral infection."

They went to the car and there was no talking, but in Lily's mind was chaos.

Hundreds of questions shot through her head: Should I tell him the truth? Could it be that it was all over, or was there still hope left?

Lily was pulled right back into reality when John touched her hand: "Darling, are you sure that everything is all right with you?"

Lily answered non chalantly: "Yes, of course, everything is all right." But she knew that nothing was all right.

CHAPTER 17

After all the secret dating with Nick, Lily realized that she had to convince John of a divorce. The only thing that Lily wanted was to be together with Nick and this time officially, without any secrets. Then they would finally make the dream of their youth come true. France was still waiting for them.

It was a beautiful day in this fall. Only some clouds were in the sky, the sun came out for a few hours and a gentle breeze was stirring. The foliage of the leaves was rotting, so that small children could play with it. When Lily woke up this morning, she knew that she would talk to John about the divorce. She had a slightly uneasy feeling. She searched almost the entire house, the bedrooms, living room, dining room, recreation room until she finally found him. He was sitting in the kitchen in front of the window watching the falling leaves. On the cooking stove which worked with coal, was sizzling a steak. Lily cleared her throat and began to speak. "John, we need to talk."

It took a few minutes before John turned around and he said nothing, just stared at Lily with large, round eyes and then he turned again to the window. Lily didn't really know what to think of it, so she mentally encouraged herself to continue. 'Go on Lily, you can do it! You are ready! Get it over with!'

Lily sat down on a chair and looked at him. She did not know how to begin. "Um, ... John, at the beginning of our marriage it was still bearable for me, but it is not anymore. And I also believe your love for me changed into hate or rather indifference."

Before she said her next sentence she waited if John showed any reaction. John was still turned towards the window. He didn't look at her, he wasn't moving, the only thing he did was breathing faintly.

So Lily went on: "I believe that it is better for both of us, if ... if we filed for a divorce! We're going to break mentally because of this convenience marriage."

John still sat on the chair in front of the window but his hands were clenching the window sill. He spoke so quietly that it was difficult to understand him. "Lily, I've always loved you, no matter how you have behaved towards me. And we both know that I am nothing more than an annoying appendage for you! Even now that you're suggesting our divorce I still love you."

His voice got louder. "When we got married it was meant 'till death do us part and only this will end our marriage! Do you understand me?"

In the meantime John was standing and had knocked over the chair on which he had been sitting. His eyes were narrow and his finger was directed threateningly at Lily.

Lily tried once more. She wanted the divorce from John, no matter what would happen. "John, don't you see how we both are breaking down. We are emotional wrecks!"

With fast and energetic steps he came up to Lily. He grabbed her by the shoulder, thus forcing her to get up and pressed her against the wall. His face in front of her, he yelled at her: "I was asking if you understand me. I know you want to get rid of me. I also know that you have an affair, you filthy, lying bitch! And believe me, if I find out who the guy is then he'll be dead faster than you can say goodbye to him!"

His hands moved to Lily's neck and she could hardly breathe anymore. John was totally out of control. Lily's queasy feeling from the morning had come true. In a low voice she tried to call for help: "John, you're hurting me! Stop it! ... HELP, HELP, HELP!!" What the two hadn't noticed was that the steak on the stove had become hotter and hotter. It slowly turned black and thick dark smoke started to rise.

At the same time Endric Bence was on his way to Lily. He wanted to spend a bit of time with her, because he was alarmed by what his sister-in-law had told him. She had asked him to have an eye on Lily. When he arrived at the house, he heard excited voices. He knocked on the door, but nobody answered, so he went straight into the garden. He was lucky, because the French windows were wide open. Endric walked into the house and followed the voices into the kitchen where he saw John and Lily wrestling. He shouted, "John, Lily, what the hell is going on?"

Neither of the two answered him nor even noticed him. Then Endric looked into Lily's face, which was filled with fear and suddenly he knew that he had to do something. So he tried to separate the two by walking between them.

When John saw him he shouted: "How did you get into my house? Go away, you have nothing to do here!"

Endric answered him: "There is no reason to hurt her, let her go! You must not treat her like this!"

Then John shouted angrily: "She's my wife, I can do what I want with her! Go out of my way!"

Endric was so annoyed by this last sentence, that he lost control and punched John into the face. John lost his balance and released Lily, who fell down. Her arm touched the pan with the steak, so that the oil spilled over. Soon it began to burn but they didn't notice it. However, Lily ran out of the kitchen, because she was afraid of her husband and heard her uncle, who told her to get help.

Confused Lily knocked on the doors of their neighbors, but even though she heard voices or saw light in the houses, no one opened the door. Nobody wanted to get involved. Tears ran down her face and she screamed for help, but nothing happened.

Meanwhile, John and Endric were fighting in the house, but they didn't realize that the house was beginning to burn.

With a bang the front windows burst and suddenly all of the main floor was ablaze. Outside, in front of her house, Lily felt powerless and desperate.

Lily was looking at the burning house. She had some bad burns but she ignored them. She hoped Endric had been able to rescue himself. In her mind different thoughts went around but she did not think about the worst. On the one hand Lily wanted the house to burn down. She wanted John dead because she wanted to forget all those things that he had done to her. On the other hand she did not want the house to burn down because of her uncle. She could not imagine that Endric had saved her life, the same one whom she had hated because he had told her father of her and Nick. But now she realized he always had only tried to protect her. He was her uncle. Who wants his own uncle to die? No one.

After some time, Lily heard the sirens of the fire-fighters and sent a prayer of thanks to God. But what she didn't know was that it was one of her neighbors, who had watched the whole situation secretly and then called the fire department.

Finally the firefighters came. She realized that she had been deep in thought.

"I wish Nick would be here right now." Then a firefighter came to her and asked her some questions, then he looked into her big green eyes and asked her: "Is anybody inside?"

Lily answered: "My uncle!" and quietly added "My husband."

After a while he said: "We are sorry, but I think we cannot save them anymore."

Suddenly she began to cry very hard. "They are dead? My uncle? My uncle and my husband? Why now?"

She became silent again.

Suddenly Lily was speaking to herself: "Maybe God wanted the house to burn down, maybe God wanted me to get free.

Now I can live with Nick. Yes, with Nick, my love. There is nothing anymore that can stop us!"

Two minutes later Nick came to the burning place. He saw that the house had burned down beyond repair. In his mind were many things. He started to shout: "Lily, Lily!" very loudly. Everyone looked at him. But Lily was dreaming and didn't hear him. Nick went to the firefighters and said: "Where is Lily?" The firefighters ignored Nick. He shouted again: "Where is Lily?" Lily noticed Nick, she said very quietly: "I am here." Nick went very fast to her and hugged her and said: "It's all over, my love." Lily answered very quietly: "My uncle and John are dead." and she began to cry hysterically.

Nick took Lily to the hospital and Lily said: "I want to go to France. All I want is to forget everything that happened here and just be with you."

CHAPTER 18

Nick and Lily were in the treatment room. Lily was lying in the hospital bed, staring at the ceiling, while Nick sat across from her and watched her. They did not speak to each other. Lily's eyes were full of tears and one could see by the expression on her face that she still didn't realize that a fatal blaze had happened. Lily's thoughts were concentrated only on the accident: 'Am I responsible for the accident? Could I have prevented it?'

Nick asked Lily: "Do you want to talk about it?"

Lily cold-heartedly replied: "There is nothing we need to talk about, leave me alone!"

Before Nick could answer, the door opened and the doctor came in. He came in with a smile and greeted them.

Nick asked him: "Dr. Demsey, is everything okay with her?"

The doctor answered: "Yes, your child is doing well!"

Nick turned his head to Lily and looked at Lily questioningly while Lily averted her eyes.

Nick said: "I thank you for the good news, Dr. Demsey."

The doctor told them that he wanted to keep Lily in the hospital for a couple of days and with a smiling face the doctor left the room.

Worried Lily looked out of the window. She couldn't say a word.

Nick cleared his throat and spoke into the silence: "Lily, you know that you owe me an explanation ... Damn, look at me!"

Touchily she replied: "What do you want me to say now?"

Then a little bit stunned and angry Nick said: "Don't you even think, that you should tell me about the child that you are expecting? When did you want to tell me about it, when you couldn't hide it no longer?"

Sarcastically Lily answered: "I'm so sorry that I didn't tell you that my husband raped me a few times and now a monster is growing in my belly. I'm really sorry! Next time I'll tell you directly, I promise!"

"Oh, Lily," was the only thing Nick could say, because Lily interrupted him and spoke again: "Oh, and now I have to explain to my child that I killed its father! And you seriously ask me why I didn't tell you?"

Enraged Nick responded to her: "You knew before yesterday that you are pregnant. You were the last person who I thought would deceive me. I always trusted you and I confided everything to you, no matter how hard it was for me!"

Full of anger Nick left the room and slammed the door. Lily shouted after him: "And now you, too!"

CHAPTER 19

For some days after this argument Nick didn't get in touch with Lily, because he needed some time to think. Nick sat on a bench in a park and the sun shone on his face. All his thoughts were about Lily and the baby.

'What shall I do now? Can I love the child of another man like my own? What does it mean for me and Lily? Is this the end of us now? Could I be its father? But Lily didn't want this pregnancy. I must be with her now; she's the love of my life! We have endured so much together and we will cope with the future. I know it! I love you, Lily!'

Smiling and determined Nick went to the hospital to Lily. He bought her a beautiful bouquet of roses. When he arrived at the hospital, he asked a nurse for Lily and she told him that Lily had been released at her own request. She gave him the tip to search at her parent's house because they had picked her up. So Nick went to the house of Lily's parents.

He knocked on the door and Lily's mother opened. She led him into the dining room. At the end of a long mahogany table Lily was sitting and as she saw him, she didn't know how to react. Her hands began to sweat and her heart beat like crazy, but she felt uncomfortable because of their last dispute. The two looked each other deep in the eyes.

Lily's mother took the word: "I'll leave you two alone. Lily, I'm right in the kitchen if something is wrong."

Nick sat down beside Lily and took her hand. He was excited, and with a trembling voice he began to speak: "Lily, please excuse my reaction, I don't know what got into me. I was overwhelmed. I couldn't think clearly. Please forgive me, I did wrong to you."

On Lily's face a smile was noticeable and the two kissed.

Then Nick went on: "Lily, please grant me the honor and become my wife. I love you, no matter what will happen. I know that you are my fate, and I am yours. I will love this child like my own. It will all be well. Trust me!"

Touched by Nick's words tears were rolling down Lily's face. She knew that he was the man of her dreams and she loved him infinitely. Quietly, she confided to him: "I do not know if I can love it …"

Lily's mother, who had overheard the entire conversation, came back into the room. She knelt in front of Lily and put her hands on Lily's knees.

"Lily, my child, I know you're in a difficult situation and it doesn't feel right to you to be pregnant, but in the course of time, you will love this child. Now that you have told me everything that happened I can understand you much better. I know that you're afraid that it will be like John, but you and Nick are better people. It cannot be like John. It will be a good person. I know it. Darling, you just have to give all your love and all will be well. Don't doubt your and Nick's ability."

Anxiously Lily looked into her mother's eyes and asked, if she was sure. Then her mother replied, "I'm your mother. I know it and if something doesn't work out, then I'm still here – I always will be," and gave her a kiss on the forehead. Lily hugged her mother first and then Nick. She was grateful for so much support from them. She again was convinced that she would be able to do it even if it would be difficult.

CHAPTER 20

Nick and Lily remained at the house of Lily's parents for a few days. Lily was much better and she slowly accepted her pregnancy.

One morning Lily was very quiet and she looked thoughtful. Nick didn't notice this and talked with Lily's mother. Suddenly Lily sat up and said: "I need to talk with you."

Lily's mother and Nick first looked questioningly at each other and then looked expectantly at Lily.

Nick asked her: "Lily, is everything all right?"

With a smile Lily answered: "Everything is well, Nick, but listen to me. Much has happened and this town is full of memories and I cannot go on as if everything is well."

Lily's mother looked sadly at her and asked: "Have I done anything wrong?"

Nick began to understand what Lily meant. He looked with a smile at Lily's mother and took her hand and said: "You did absolutely nothing wrong, my dear. I think what Lily means is that we need a new beginning!"

Lily was smiling and some tears were forming in her eyes. "We need a new home!"

Lily's Mother quickly answered: "That is not a problem, we'll search for a house for you two."

Lily replied:"No, mom, not only for a house. We need a new country!"

Lily's mother looked shocked and she tried to talk them out of this idea and suggested to search for another solution but it didn't work. Lily and Nick did not need to talk about which country. Their choice was France. They now would fulfill their biggest dream.

A few days later Lily and Nick started packing. Lily's mother accepted their decision in the course of time and helped them with the packing.

Although Lily's father was not convinced of his daughter's decision to immigrate to France, he accepted it. He also finally accepted Nick as Lily's partner because Nick had won him over because of his years in the military and the prestige he had gained there. Nick was no longer the poor neighbor's son for Lily's father; he was a man who would give his life for his country. Between Nick and him a friendship had started to develop. And Lily had also forgiven her father.

One morning the time of departure had finally come. After the last family breakfast Lily's parents brought them to the train station that would take them to the harbour. With tears Lily and her parents hugged each other for a long time.

Lily and Nick boarded the train and waved for a last time. That day they took the last train to Paris.

As the train pulled out of the station Lily looked at Nick and said: "Now we start a new life, Nick."

Nick smiled at her and answered: "Yes darling, a new life in Paris!"

Lily leaned against him and looked at her belly with a smile.